HOW WILL I KNOW WHEN YOUR FEELINGS ARE HURT?

BY Jeannette Sabatini

© 2013 by Jeannette Sabatini

All rights reserved. No part of this publication may be reproduced, stored in a retrieval system, or transmitted in any form or by any means - for example, electronic, photocopy, and recording- without the prior written permission of the publisher.

ISBN-10: 0692570152
ISBN-13: 978-0692570159 (nettesfeathers)

Dedication

This book is dedicated to children everywhere,
and to my family, particularly my husband and sons,
who are inspirational and supportive.

How will I know when your feelings are hurt?

How will I know when you're feeling like dirt?

I guess I could tell by the look on your face...

..the look that's there when I lose grace.

It's the look of sadness when I squish your lunch.

I know it will happen, cause I've done that a bunch!

It's always there when I call you that name.

You always cry! It's always the same!

I'm really tired of seeing those looks...

You look much better with a big smile!

It's usually there and it stays for a while!

I wish I could have a smile like that...

...the one that's gone when I steal your hat!

It's gone in a flash when I don't say "Hi!" back.

You keep on trying, but I'm out of whack.

Deep down, I want to be someone you like...

...who no longer says: "Go take a hike!"

So, how will I know
when I'm crossing the line?
I'll look at your face
because it's like a sign!

When I see tears
or a really big frown,
it might be because
I'm putting you down!

A smile will tell me
I'm doing okay,
and that I'm watching
the things that I say!

So, I'll look for the signs,
and then I will know,
the things that will help
a new friendship grow!

About Have a Bully-Free Day! Books

Have a Bully-Free Day! books are written to help children have a bully-free day every day at school or in the neighborhood. They build empathy and compassion and explain the rewards of being nice and the consequences of being mean. *Have a Bully-Free Day!* books help children:

- realize how negative behavior can impact friendships
- see the benefits of being friendly and positive
- welcome others into friendships
- stop seeing other kids as a threat
- deal with a person who is bullying
- be sensitive to the circumstances of others
- notice the physical signs that they have hurt another's feelings.

Kids enjoy these books because they relate to the situations presented and they enjoy the fun rhyming pattern in each. They are great for sharing: teachers can share them with a class, a counselor with a group or individual, and an older class buddy with a younger class buddy.

The author, Jeannette Sabatini, has a degree in English/Journalism. She has been an editor and writer in the medical field, but her experience as a mom and an elementary school aide inspired her to start writing and illustrating stories for children. She expresses her motherly advice through poetry.

This and other *Have a Bully-Free Day!* books are available on Amazon Books.

www.ingramcontent.com/pod-product-compliance
Lightning Source LLC
Chambersburg PA
CBHW041232040426
42444CB00002B/136